HOME IS
CALLING

For Sayra and Cheyli, their sisters and brothers,
and their very brave mama.
—K.P.

For my niece Kamila, our beautiful mariposa.
—E.P.

ISBN: 978-1-5460-0313-7

WorthyKids
Hachette Book Group
1290 Avenue of the Americas
New York, NY 10104

Library of Congress Cataloging-in-Publication Data
Names: Pryor, Katherine, author. | Peterson, Ellie, illustrator.
Title: Home is calling : the journey of the monarch butterfly / written by
   Katherine Pryor ; illustrated by Ellie Peterson.
Description: First edition. | New York, NY : WorthyKids/Hachette Book
   Group, [2023] | Audience: Ages 4-7 | Summary: "An illustrated story
   written from the point of view of monarch butterflies as they search for
   food and fly through storms during their annual migration"—Provided by
   publisher.
Identifiers: LCCN 2022045051 | ISBN 9781546003137 (hardcover)
Subjects: LCSH: Monarch butterfly—Migration—North America—Juvenile
   literature. | Monarch butterfly—Migration—Mexico—Michoacán de
   Ocampo—Juvenile literature.
Classification: LCC QL561.N9 P79 2023 | DDC
   595.78/91568097—dc23/eng/20221003
LC record available at https://lccn.loc.gov/2022045051

Designed by Melissa Reagan

Printed and bound in China • APS
10 9 8 7 6 5 4 3 2 1

HOME IS CALLING

The Journey of the Monarch Butterfly

By Katherine Pryor
Art by Ellie Peterson

The Journey

Every fall, monarch caterpillars hatch in the
eastern United States and southern Canada before
undertaking an amazing journey of up to three
thousand miles south to winter in the mountain forests
of central Mexico. It takes four generations for the
monarchs leaving Mexico in the spring to reach their
northern destination, but the monarchs traveling south
fly the entire way.

Birds sing.

The sun peeks over the lake.

It's time to...

go!

Our wings beat an orange-and-black kaleidoscope against a blue sky.
We catch a southward wind and soar away from the place we were born
and into the first day of our journey to our new home.

HOME IS CALLING.

Our great-great-grandparents
left their home forest in Mexico
seven months ago, so we could
hatch in Canada. Soon it will
be too cold here, and we must
return without them.

Not all of us will make it,
but we will try.

We glide until the sun grows hot on our wings,
then dip to earth to sip sweet nectar from a
patch of wildflowers.

The sun sets.

We roost together
in a sugar maple tree
for the night.

The sun rises.

We fly.

Sunset.

Sunrise.

Sunset.

Sunrise.

For days and days
and days,

we fly.

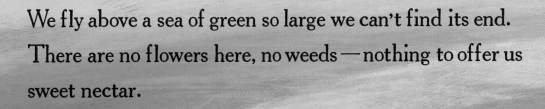

We fly above a sea of green so large we can't find its end. There are no flowers here, no weeds — nothing to offer us sweet nectar.

Some of us grow so tired and hungry that our wings cease to beat, and we fall to the ground below.

Finally, we spot a splash of yellow, then a rainbow of flowers. A feast! We dive toward the food, proboscises probing. We drink, then rest in an apple tree.

H.G.G. ELEMENTARY

At dawn, we fly again.

HOME IS CALLING.

The wind grows fierce.

Dark clouds roll toward us.

The air turns cold.

We must find shelter.

But the sea of green continues below. We need a patch of
strong trees to shelter us from the storm. The wind grabs
at our wings, pulling some of us down to earth.
There! A stand of oak trees on the edge of a field.

We cling to the limbs beneath their broad leaves as raindrops turn to hail. The wind howls and screams. We huddle together to protect each other from the storm.

When the sun shines once more,
we stretch our wings and soar.

HOME IS CALLING.

We fly along rivers, over mountains, and around cities.
We rest in trees, gardens, and roadside ditches.

Cool fall air
chases us south.

Have we chosen
the wrong path?

We've never been
to our new home.

How will we know
when we've found it?

After two long months, a desert stretches before us.
We start to lose hope. Then, finally, things begin to feel ... familiar.
Is that a glint of sunlight on a mountaintop?
Is that a green grove of fir trees?

We sense we are close, just as our ancestors
and their ancestors knew when they were close.

Antennae twitching in anticipation, we circle the forest,
searching for a safe place to land. Jagged stumps line the forest floor.

Where are the trees?
Our home is gone.

Some of us dip and drop with sadness.
Others fly up, up, up to get a better view.

In the distance, fir trees glow orange as if on fire.
But that is no fire.

Those are monarchs!

We ride the wind toward these distant relatives we
have never met. We circle the grove, settling onto tall firs.

Safe at last in our new home.

Anatomy of a Butterfly

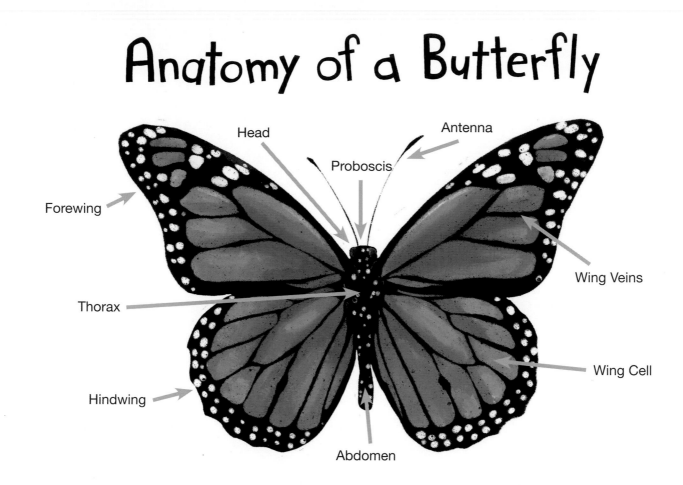

Head

Antenna

Proboscis

Forewing

Wing Veins

Thorax

Hindwing

Wing Cell

Abdomen

Life Cycle

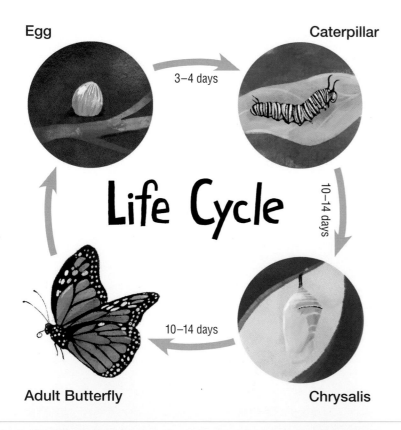

Egg

Caterpillar

3–4 days

10–14 days

Adult Butterfly

10–14 days

Chrysalis

Insects change form as they grow in a process called metamorphosis. Monarch butterflies will pass through four distinct stages during this process.

Egg. An adult female monarch lays an egg on a milkweed leaf. She repeats this process to lay hundreds of eggs in her lifetime.

Caterpillar. A larva, or caterpillar, eats its way out of the shell and feeds on milkweed until it grows to many times its original size. It molts, or sheds its skin, as it grows.

Chrysalis. The caterpillar crawls away from the milkweed and weaves a silk pad to hang from. It molts one last time to reveal the chrysalis, or pupa.

Butterfly. A fully formed monarch emerges from the chrysalis. It rests in a protected area while its wings dry and harden, then flies off in search of nectar.

Milkweed, Marvelous Milkweed

Milkweed is a beautiful flowering plant that serves as a host plant for monarch butterflies. Adult monarchs rely on milkweed nectar, while milkweed leaves are the only plant monarch caterpillars eat. Chemicals within the milkweed leaves make adult monarch butterflies taste bad to most predators, which helps to keep the butterflies safe.

Threats to Monarchs

Sadly, monarch populations have declined by eighty percent since the 1990s. Some places consider milkweed a noxious weed and have worked to eradicate it by spraying chemical herbicides on farms and along roads. This has eliminated the monarch caterpillars' only source of food, which is disastrous for the butterflies. The loss of blooming weeds and wildflowers makes it difficult for adult monarchs to find nectar. Climate change is causing extreme temperatures and powerful storms, and illegal logging in the monarchs' home forest in central Mexico means that monarchs have fewer trees to winter in.

Get Involved

You can help scientists as they study and track monarch butterflies.

♦ **Order** milkweed plugs or learn how to create a Monarch Waystation at MonarchWatch.org.

♦ **Report** monarch egg, larvae, and butterfly sightings at JourneyNorth.org.

♦ If you are in California, **sign up** for the Xerces Society Thanksgiving and New Year's Monarch Counts at WesternMonarchCount.org.

♦ **Explore** opportunities through the National Wildlife Federation at NWF.org or contact your local wildlife organizations.

Migratory Groups

The eastern migratory monarch travels from the Great Lakes region of the United States and Canada to winter in Mexico each fall, a trip of up to three thousand miles. The western migratory monarch travels from west of the Rocky Mountains to winter on the California coast. There is evidence that some eastern monarchs end up in California—further proof of these tiny creatures' amazing abilities.

Monarch Migration

- Overwintering areas
- Spring breeding areas
- Spring and summer breeding areas
- Summer breeding areas
- Nonmigratory population
- Fall migration path
- Spring migration path
- Potential monarch breeding habitat

How Do They Do It?

Scientists believe that monarch butterflies rely on solar angles and magnetic forces. Monarchs travel alone during the day, but often roost together at night. People report seeing monarchs roost in the same trees year after year, even though that generation of monarchs has never been there before. Even monarchs hatched in a lab will find their way back to the same forest as their ancestors.

A Note from the Author

In 2022, migratory monarch butterflies were classified as endangered by the International Union for Conservation of Nature. Both the eastern migratory monarch and the western migratory monarch are experiencing tragic declines in their numbers.

Endangered means something is in danger of disappearing forever. No one would ever witness the monarchs' amazing journey again. However, humans have worked with nature to save endangered creatures in the past, and we can do it again. Protecting migratory monarchs will require cooperation, dedication, and a willingness to create changes to protect their migration paths.

You Can Help!

- **Plant** native milkweed so monarch butterflies have more places to lay eggs, and so caterpillars have a food source. Milkweed can be poisonous to animals, so it's important to plant milkweed in a place where it won't be nibbled by other unsuspecting animals.

- **Start** a pesticide-free butterfly garden at home or school to provide adult butterflies with sources of nectar.

- **Ask** your local city council or parks department to stop using chemical herbicides to kill flowering weeds in parks, roadsides, or other important natural spaces.

The good news? Helping monarch butterflies protects so many other species! Creating a healthier world for monarchs benefits countless other butterflies, birds, bees, moths, and insects. We humans can do a lot of good when we put our minds and hearts to it, but the time to act is now.